HOW TO MAKE MONEY AND LOSE WEIGHT

HOW TO MAKE MONEY AND LOSE WEIGHT

A Simple Guide for Everyone

by
Babe Lincoln

✿

EXTREMEINK BOOKS
LOS ANGELES, CALIFORNIA

How to Make Money and Lose Weight
By Babe Lincoln

Copyright © 2009 by Babe Lincoln

This book is intended for reference and entertainment purposes only. It is not a medical manual. Investments in the stock market may lose value. Money market funds are not guaranteed or insured by the United States government.

Mention of specific brand-name products, books, companies, organizations, authors or authorities in this book does not imply endorsement by the author or publisher, nor does mention of specific brand-name products, books, companies, organizations, authors or authorities imply that they endorse this book, its author, or the publisher. The brand-name products mentioned in this book are trademarks or registered trademarks of their respective companies.

Internet addresses given in this book were accurate at the time of publication.

Published by ExtremeInk Books
www.ExtremeInk.com

Printed in the United States of America

First edition.

Library of Congress Control Number: 2009902179

ISBN-13: 978-0-9823837-0-4
ISBN-10: 0-9823837-0-3

Acknowledgments

The author would like to thank Susan Shelley for editorial assistance, and for personally having almost all the learning experiences that were the basis for this book.

Thanks also to Argus Hamilton for encouragement, friendship, and the fake ID.

In memory of R.R.,
who said,
"It CAN be done."

Contents

Introduction

The thing to remember, if you want to make money and lose weight, is that you are perfectly capable of doing it without any help from anybody.

You don't need a financial adviser, or a diet counselor, or any of the people who are paid a handsome commission to convince you that you can't do this yourself.

You *can* do it yourself.

But no one's going to make any money telling you *that*.

The truth hurts, if you're on commission.

Part 1

How to Make Money

"I couldn't wait for success, so I went ahead without it."

— *Jonathan Winters*

1

How to Make Money

The easiest, safest, surest way to make money is to invest your extra cash over time in a diversified portfolio of high-quality stocks, always paying a price-per-share that is lower than average.

This technique is called dollar-cost averaging.

Small investors can reap the benefits of dollar-cost averaging by investing in a low-cost mutual fund.

It works like this: You open your account with the minimum investment, generally between $3,000 and $10,000, then invest a fixed amount every month, let's say $100, from the extra cash you'd otherwise spend on things you'll never miss.

Every month, your hundred dollars will buy a different quantity of shares.

When the price of the shares is higher, your money will buy fewer of them.

When the price of the shares is lower, your money will buy more of them.

Over time, you will pay a price-per-share that is lower than average.

It's simple math.

The key is to do this with money you're sure you won't need in the next five years. The market fluctuates, sometimes sickeningly, and it's important to be able to wait patiently and not put yourself under pressure to sell.

Keep your short-term, pay-the-bills-in-an-emergency cash in a money market account.

Only invest the money you're sure you won't need any-time soon.

When you open your account, take advantage of the op-tion to reinvest the dividends and capital gains. That will help your investment grow more quickly. Then, every month, invest an additional $100. It's not a bad idea to set up an automatic investment from your checking account. We all mean well.

Over time, dollar-cost averaging will turn $100 a month in spare cash into something big enough to solve a real problem. It could help you buy a car, make a down payment on a house, pay for college, or give you the confidence you need to take a career risk.

Dollar-cost averaging frees you from the stress of trying to time the market, and mutual fund investing frees you from the stress of trying to pick stocks.

In good markets, you accumulate shares slowly and sleep through the night.

In bad markets, you remember that you're buying shares at a discount, kind of like a sale at Bloomingdale's, and you fall right back to sleep.

Next, you need a good, low-cost mutual fund.

"Everyone has the brainpower to follow the stock market. If you made it through fifth-grade math, you can do it."

— Peter Lynch

2
Picking a Mutual Fund

A mutual fund is a company that buys a mix of investment products and sells shares of its mix to investors. Every share of a mutual fund includes a tiny percentage of everything the fund owns. It's a way for small investors to get the benefits of diversification.

Mutual fund companies charge fees for this service, so it's important to know what you're paying and what you're getting.

Or you could save yourself the headache and invest in an index fund.

Index funds seek to mimic the performance of a stock market index by owning the stocks that make up the index.

For example, if you invest in the Vanguard 500 Index Fund or the Fidelity Spartan 500 Index Fund, your returns will track with the S&P 500, an index made up of the stocks of 500 large companies.

The Fidelity Spartan Total Market Index Fund seeks to mirror the total return of the Wilshire 5000 index, which aims to reflect the performance of the entire stock market, both big companies and smaller ones.

Similarly, the Vanguard Total Stock Market Index Fund tracks the performance of the MSCI U.S. Broad Market Index, which includes approximately 3,900 U.S. companies of all sizes and represents about 99.5% of the total U.S. stock market.

Index funds have very low expenses because they don't have a fund manager who's picking stocks and running up the fund's expenses with a lot of buying and selling.

And expenses matter.

How much?

Let's say you want to invest $5,000 in a mutual fund, and you've narrowed your choices down to three.

Your first choice, an index fund, has no sales charge and annual expenses of 0.1%.

Your second choice, an actively managed fund, has no sales charge and annual expenses of 2%.

Your third choice, a fund highly recommended by a broker, has a sales charge of 6%, a deferred sales charge—that's a sales charge you pay when you sell—of 2%, and annual expenses of 3.5%.

Let's assume that all three funds have an annual return of 5%. How much money would your $5,000 investment be worth at the end of five years?

According to the Mutual Fund Cost Calculator on the web site of the U.S. Securities and Exchange Commission (**www.sec.gov**):

♦ The index fund would be worth $6,349.56.

♦ The actively managed fund would be worth $5,768.29.

♦ The fund recommended by the broker would be worth $4,919.74.

Of course, any broker would tell you that the fund he or she recommended will do a lot better than those other funds you're considering.

Even if that's true, and it might not be, here's the thing to remember: The fund can do better and *you* can still do worse.

The broker-recommended fund could beat the index fund's performance and still not return as much money to you, the investor, because of its sales charge, deferred sales charge, and higher annual expenses.

The broker's fund in our example could have a return of 6% per year, and at the end of five years your $5,000 investment would be worth $5,163.37.

It could have a return of 7% per year, and at the end of five years you'd have $5,416.37.

Even if it had a return of 10% a year, *double* the performance of the stock market index in our example, it would still only be worth $6,234.29 after five years, and your index fund would have beaten it by more than a hundred dollars.

Sales charges and fees are not a guarantee that you're paying for quality. They don't fall into the "you get what you pay for" category.

Sales charges and fees pay for brokers' commissions, glossy brochures full of bar charts, and expensive advertising campaigns that make you feel like it's all just too complicated for you to understand without professional advisers.

But now that you understand, you can do without their advice.

Which brings us to the most important advice of all.

3
Lincoln's Law

The more money they're spending to sell it to you, the less you need it.

"The way to get started is to quit talking and begin doing."

— *Walt Disney*

4
How to Get Started

Once you know what you're looking for, you can easily find all the information you need.

If you'd like to invest in a Vanguard or Fidelity index fund, go to **www.Vanguard.com** or **www.Fidelity.com** to review and download information, including a prospectus and application form. Or call the companies directly: Vanguard's toll-free phone number is 877-662-7447, and Fidelity's is 800-343-3548. You don't need a broker.

Now you can skip ahead to the next chapter.

If you'd like to look a little further for more mutual fund choices, you can find information and performance history data at **http://finance.yahoo.com**, at the web sites of major newspapers, and in many other places around the Internet.

Sometimes it's easier to compare mutual funds on paper. USA Today and the Wall Street Journal carry comprehensive reports on mutual fund performance at the end of every quarter. Mark your calendar for the end of March, June, September and December and watch for the quarterly mutual fund performance issues.

Here are some tips on what to look for when you look:

♦ Check to make sure there's **no sales charge**, also called a "load," on the front end or the back end.

♦ Check to make sure there's **no 12b-1 fee**. Named for the SEC rule that allows it, a 12b-1 fee pays for marketing to new investors at the expense of current investors. If you see a really impressive TV commercial for a mutual fund company, look up their fees and see who's paying for it.

♦ Compare the **expense ratios** of the funds you're considering. Lower is better. You really don't want to pay more than 1%.

♦ Look at the five-year and, if it's available, the **ten-year performance record** of the fund. There are many factors in the market, like the direction of interest rates or the strength of the dollar against other currencies, that can boost a fund's performance in the short term but are unlikely to be repeated anytime soon. Beware of funds that have had an uncharacteristically big move up in the last year; their next big move could be down.

♦ Check the **portfolio turnover rate**. Lower is better. A high portfolio turnover rate means the fund manager is doing a lot of buying and selling, which raises the fund's expenses and also may increase your tax liability. The capital gains generated by a mutual fund are paid out to the shareholders and you may have to pay tax on that money, even if you reinvested it to buy more shares.

♦ Check the **minimum initial investment** and the **minimum new investment**. Some funds will allow you to invest as little as $100 per month, and others will have higher minimums. You can always invest quarterly instead of monthly if you choose a fund with a higher minimum for additional investments.

"Be not afraid of going slowly, be afraid only of standing still."

— *Chinese proverb*

5
Relax

That's all there is to it.

- ◆ Pick a good, low-cost mutual fund.

- ◆ Open an account with the minimum investment.

- ◆ Reinvest the dividends and capital gains.

- ◆ Add a fixed amount to your investment every month with an automatic withdrawal from your checking account.

Then forget about it.

Don't be panicked if the market goes down, don't be manic if the market goes up. You're a long-term investor. Remember, the money you put in the market should be money you're pretty sure you won't need for at least five years.

Keep investing. Every month. In good markets and in bad markets.

Save your statements in a file. You'll need them for tax accounting, eventually. When you sell, the price you paid for the shares will be used to calculate your capital gains.

The sooner you start, the better you'll end up.

"We made too many wrong mistakes."

— *Yogi Berra*

6
Winning by Not Losing

While it's great to know how to make money, it's equally useful to know how not to lose it.

The next eight chapters are not intended to give you a comprehensive understanding of every type of investment and financial instrument.

They're intended to highlight the things most likely to make you say, after it's too late, "I wish I would have known about that before."

"If at first you don't succeed, try, try again. Then quit. There's no point in being a damn fool about it."

  — *W.C. Fields*

7
How to Lose Money on Stocks

The easiest way to lose money on individual stocks is to buy them.

You can also lose money on stocks by shorting them, by buying and selling options on them, and by borrowing money against them, but the easiest way is just to buy them.

It may seem that some people are experts at picking stocks, or that some people are handing out hot tips about stocks that are poised to rise, but the truth is that nobody knows what will go up and what will go down.

Information moves so quickly that every tiny fragment of fact or rumor is immediately priced into the stocks, and there is no reason to believe that anyone is telling you something that everyone doesn't already know.

So in the stock market, everybody knows everything, and nobody knows anything.

Or, as Princeton University economics professor Burton Malkiel wrote in his 1973 book, *A Random Walk Down Wall Street*, in theory a blindfolded monkey throwing darts at a newspaper's financial pages can put together a portfolio that will do just as well as any expert's.

He never did explain why you have to blindfold the monkey.

The point is that there are no hot tips that will make you a sure-thing fortune. It is much more likely that the person calling you with the hot tip is trying to unload shares of stock that are nearly certain to go down in value, and quickly.

Always consider the possibility that the person calling you with the tip has been heavily incentivized by his or her employer to sell you those shares.

Stockbrokers receive a commission on everything they sell to you and everything they sell for you.

Sometimes stockbrokers will offer to buy you lunch or dinner so they can discuss ways for you to reach your financial goals.

Do not accept this offer.

Free meals are a dead giveaway.

It's Lincoln's Law in action: The more money they're spending to sell it to you, the less you need it.

"Man, I really like Vegas."
    — Elvis Presley

8

How to Lose Money on Options, Commodities, and Sports Betting

If you want to lose money really fast, you can't do better than options and commodities trading.

You could go to Las Vegas and throw it down on a roulette table, but the casino will buy you dinner at the buffet, so it won't be a total loss.

Some kinds of investing are really just different forms of gambling. You're placing a bet that on a particular date, the price of a security or commodity will be higher or lower than it is right now.

Gambling can be fun and exciting, and it always looks like someone nearby is winning big.

There's just one problem.

Math.

Sometimes you'll win and sometimes you'll lose. But you'll almost always win less money when you win than you'll lose when you lose.

For example, if you bet a thousand dollars in order to win two hundred, and you win four bets in a row, you're up eight hundred dollars. But if you lose the fifth bet, that thousand dollars you just lost wipes out all your winnings.

You won four out of five bets. You won *80 percent of the time*. And you still lost $200.

Watch out for that.

"This used to be a government of checks and balances. Now it's all checks and no balances."

— *Gracie Allen*

9

How to Lose Money on Bonds

A bond is a promise to pay. When you buy a bond, you're loaning money to the issuer of the bond, which may be a company or a government entity. The bond is a pledge to pay you back, and to pay you interest on your money at a rate that's set when the bond is issued.

Bonds can be confusing because after they are issued they are freely traded in the market, and their prices fluctuate with various market conditions.

Even if a bond is guaranteed by the full faith and credit of the United States government, the value of the bond may still decline. That's because the risk of default is not the only factor making the bond market exciting. The big risk is interest rates.

Let's say you buy a bond with a 5% interest rate and a year later you want to sell it, but during the year interest rates have gone up and similar bonds now pay 7%.

Your bond is worth less than you paid for it. You've got a piece of paper that spits nickels, and anybody can walk up to the counter and buy a brand new piece of paper that spits seven cents.

On the other hand, suppose you buy a bond with a 7% interest rate and a year later interest rates drop to 5%.

Your bond is now worth more. You've got a piece of paper that spits seven cents while all the new models spit nickels.

It's surprisingly easy to lose money by investing in bonds.

Suppose you're reading the financial news and you see that bonds have had a great year. Mutual funds that own bonds are at the top of the charts. The performance numbers are very impressive for every type of bond investment you see.

Then you see that you can buy bonds that are insured, guaranteed, or backed by the full faith and credit of the U.S. government.

Doesn't that sound great?

You found an investment that's safe, secure, and at the top of every list of top-performing investments for the last year.

Don't reach for your wallet just yet.

When interest rates drop, all the existing bonds with higher interest rates go up in value. So all the mutual funds that hold bonds have an impressive run up at the same time.

But if you buy a bond fund at this point, after interest rates have dropped, you might be in for a rude shock. The next interest rate move might be up, not down.

And when interest rates go up, all the existing bonds with lower interest rates are worth less. So all the bond funds go down at the same time.

Beware of buying bonds at the end of a downward move in interest rates. You could be buying at the high. Your investment will lose value when rates go up, and even with a Treasury bill there's no guarantee against that.

*"There are worse things in life
than death. Have you ever spent
an evening with an insurance
salesman?"*

— *Woody Allen*

10
How to Lose Money
on Annuities

An annuity is an insurance contract. You give the insurance company money, and they agree to make a payment or payments to you at a later date.

There are various tax laws and various circumstances that make annuities a good investment for some people and a terrible investment for others.

This is a distinction that is often lost on people who sell annuities.

Perhaps you've received one of their invitations to a financial seminar that includes a free steak dinner at an expensive restaurant.

Live by Lincoln's Law and buy your own steak dinner.

Whether annuities are right for you is beyond the scope of this book, but one key thing to watch is the surrender charge.

If you buy an annuity and you need your money out in the first five years, you may have to forfeit a great big chunk of your investment. That's because the insurance company that sold the annuity gave a great big chunk of your money to the people who bought you that free steak dinner.

Save yourself some grief and don't take financial advice from people who are trying to sell you something. They may not give you truthful or complete answers. Do your own research, or call an independent Certified Public Accountant and pay for tax advice on different types of investments. Or go back to the beginning of this book and follow the directions to dollar-cost average into a no-load mutual fund.

The money you save will be your own.

*"I'm living so far beyond my income
that we may almost be said to be
living apart."*

— *e. e. cummings*

11

How to Lose Money
in Real Estate

The easiest way to lose money in real estate is to suck all the equity out of the property if the value of the property rises.

If the value of the property then falls, you'll owe more money on the property than it's worth, and if for any reason you can't make the mortgage payments, you won't be able to sell it for enough to cover what you'll owe when you hand over the keys.

So it's risky to open all those letters from mortgage brokers and finance companies offering to help you refinance your house and take cash out for a tropical vacation or a new kitchen.

A less visible way to suck the equity out of the property is to sign up for a loan that has something called "negative amortization." That means your monthly mortgage payment is artificially low, and the difference between what you're paying and what your payment *would* be (if it wasn't artificially low) is added on to the mortgage loan every month.

Every month.

Every month the principal balance on your loan is going up, not down.

You're paying and paying and you owe more and more.

Of course, you get to live in the house, and you're paying an artificially low monthly payment that makes it much more affordable in the short term.

But keep an eye on that principal balance, because if it goes higher than the property is worth, you're upside-down, and you won't be able to sell the place for what you owe on it in case you need to get out in a hurry.

If that happens, you'll have two choices: pay the bank the difference between the sale price and what you owe on the mortgage, or default on the loan and let the bank take the property in a foreclosure.

If you go into foreclosure, your credit score will be hammered. That will make all your financial transactions more difficult and more expensive in the future.

You may even owe income tax on the part of the mortgage loan that went unpaid. It could be considered a gift to you from your mortgage lender.

Bet you didn't even know they cared.

*"The salesman knows nothing
of what he is selling save that he
is charging a great deal too
much for it."*

— *Oscar Wilde*

12
How to Lose Money on Cars

It's easy to lose money on a new car because cars depreciate so sharply the moment you drive them off the dealer's lot.

The cost of repairs and body work, however, starts high and gets higher the longer you own your car.

So the easiest way to lose money with a car—short of driving it to a seminar on annuities—is to take out a four-year or five-year loan on a new car and then have a wreck that totals the car during the first two years.

If that happens, your insurance company will write you a check for the current value of the car, which may not be enough to pay off the loan. Regardless of what they pay you,

you'll still have to pay off the loan and buy another car at the same time.

To minimize the risk of that happening, get the shortest-term loan you can possibly afford and stay in the right-hand lane until it's paid off.

You can lose money on an old car, too. All you have to do is pay your insurance company for collision coverage without checking to see if the value of the car has fallen below the likely repair cost for a minor fender-bender. If it has, the insurance company won't pay for the repairs to your beloved vehicle. They'll just call it names and write you a check for a tiny fraction of what you paid them in premiums for collision coverage you mistakenly thought you had.

Don't expect your insurance company to volunteer this information. Call them up and ask them about it before you have the fender-bender and the name-calling starts.

It's also easy to lose money on a rental car. If you sign up for the rental car company's collision damage waiver and other coverage without checking to see if your credit card already gives you that insurance, you can pay high fees for something you don't need at all.

The next time you rent a car, call your credit card company before you go to pick up the vehicle. You may be able to decline the car company's insurance in complete serenity.

"I'm proud to pay taxes in the United States; the only thing is, I could be just as proud for half the money."

— *Arthur Godfrey*

13

How to Lose Money in a 401(k) Account

A 401(k) account is a tax-deferred investment account that employers can offer their employees, and if you have one, you probably have already discovered five or six different ways to lose money in them.

But in addition to the investment risk of the various choices offered to you, there is another way to lose money in a 401(k).

Borrow from it.

Many 401(k) plans allow employees to loan themselves money from their account, which sounds like a pretty good deal because the borrower is paying interest to himself for the use of the money. But if the loan isn't paid back at some point, the IRS considers it a withdrawal, and that turns the amount of the loan into income, and that means the borrower has to come up with money to pay the taxes on the money that was borrowed, which of course is long gone.

The IRS may also hit you with a penalty for an early withdrawal from a tax-deferred account, unless you're old enough to get away with it.

Borrowing from a 401(k) is a good way to lose money for another reason, too: if you're making loan payments, you're probably not making new investments, which means you're losing the opportunity to have your employer match your contributions, and you're losing the effect of compounding on all the money that's not going in.

And, of course, if you lose your job while you owe money to your 401(k), everything gets even worse.

Don't borrow from your 401(k) for anything less than a real emergency. Otherwise the final touch on the remodeling of the bathrooms could be a spectacular spin down the drain.

*"Man is the only animal that can be
skinned more than once."*

— *Jimmy Durante*

14

How to Lose Money
with Credit Cards

The quickest way to lose money with credit cards is to pay
them late.

Don't pay them late. Not even one day late. Not ever.

Even if you owe just a tiny minimum payment of $15, a
credit card company will blow you up if you fail to pay it.

You will see your interest rate skyrocket from an affordable seven or ten or fifteen percent to an insane 35 percent,
plus late charges.

That credit card balance you're carrying will blast off like a
NASA rocket when 35 percent interest makes contact with it.

Even worse, all your other credit cards will get the word
about the late payment and jack up your interest rate as well.
They all belong to the same union.

Missing a payment is a sure-fire way to lose money with credit cards, but there are other methods, too.

Sometimes a credit card company will offer you a promotional balance transfer with a low interest rate. Only accept this offer if your current balance on this card is zero, and then do not use this credit card for any other purchases.

That's because every payment you make will be applied to the promotional balance transfer amount until it's completely paid off. Any other balance on that card will accrue interest at a higher rate in the meantime.

So you'll be paying a high rate of interest on that previous balance, or on that dinner or bar tab or gasoline bill, until the end of time.

If you're carrying a credit card balance, it's a good idea to have another card that you pay off every month. That's the card you should use for restaurants and bars and other things that you might otherwise pay for with cash.

Don't fall into the trap of carrying a balance on a card that gives you airline miles or promotional gifts. Every time you charge something new on that card, you'll be paying high interest charges on that purchase. Those free airline tickets and binoculars are no bargain unless you pay off the credit card bill every month.

Conclusion

The trick to making money is to invest steadily and prudently and patiently in things you understand.

Experts may tell you they know many other tricks.

Sure they do.

Use your own judgment. There's nothing wrong with it.

Part 2

How to Lose Weight

"The first step towards getting somewhere is to decide that you are not going to stay where you are."

— *Chauncey Depew*

1
You Can Do This

Anyone, at any age, can lose weight.

It isn't necessary to spend any money on diet programs, special food, counseling, fitness coaches, or psychotherapy.

All you need to lose weight is information and simple math.

You need to know how many calories your body burns in your normal daily activities.

You need to know how many calories you consume in your normal daily meals.

You need to make the second number lower than the first number.

Of course, people can make weight loss seem more complicated. That's how they make money selling diet programs, special food, counseling, fitness coaching and psychotherapy.

Live by Lincoln's Law: The more money they're spending to sell it to you, the less you need it.

The worst thing about most diet advice, paid and unpaid, is that it makes you feel like there's something really wrong with you just because you have some weight to lose. You have to change your habits. You have to change your schedule. You have to get out of your self-destructive patterns. You have to confront the problems that are making you stressed. You have to eat when you're not hungry and not eat when you are. You have to exercise an hour a day, three times a week.

In other words, you have to become an entirely different person.

No, you don't.

You just have eat 500 calories a day less than your body burns.

That's it. That's all.

"Diets, like clothes, should be tailored to you."

— Joan Rivers

2
Simple Math

If you pick up a package of anything edible in the grocery store, you'll find a nutritional information label that lists the "Percent Daily Values" of the product's fat, carbohydrate, protein, and vitamin content. Then, in very small print, you'll see this qualifier: "Percent Daily Values are based on a 2,000 calorie diet. Your daily values may be higher or lower depending on your calorie needs."

Chances are good, especially if you're female, that you don't burn 2,000 calories a day. Your body may burn 1,500. If you eat a 2,000-calorie daily diet, you will gain a pound a week.

That's because a pound of fat is 3,500 calories. Five hundred excess calories in your diet every day will total 3,500 excess calories every week and you will gain about four pounds a month.

So if you're currently gaining weight at the rate of a pound a week, you don't need a diet counselor, just a calculator. Find five hundred calories a day that you can cut out of your diet, and you will stop gaining weight even if you don't exercise or change your lifestyle in any other way.

If your weight is currently stable but you'd like to lose some of it, find five hundred calories a day that you can cut out of your diet and you will lose a pound a week.

Guaranteed.

No therapy required.

Where you cut those calories is entirely up to you. And you don't have to cut them from the same place all the time. If you'd rather give up beer than French fries, or if you'd rather give up French fries than beer, or if you'd rather keep them both and skip breakfast, it's nobody else's business but yours.

Eat 500 calories a day below what your body burns and you'll lose a pound a week. Or cut just 250 calories a day and lose half a pound per week.

Slowly, steadily, comfortably, inexpensively, and privately, you will lose weight.

It's simple math.

"He who hesitates is sometimes saved."
     — *James Thurber*

3
A Word about Health

Don't do anything stupid.

Don't fast, don't use laxatives or diuretics as diet aids, don't smoke, don't take amphetamines, don't ignore your body's warnings if you don't feel well, and don't rush into any diet or exercise program without checking with your doctor, especially if you have any issues with your health.

Try to eat a reasonably balanced diet over the long term. It's possible to lose weight eating nothing but candy bars and diet soda, but, you know, it's not really good for you.

"In two decades I've lost a total of 789 pounds. I should be hanging from a charm bracelet."

— *Erma Bombeck*

4
Burning Up

How many calories does your body burn, and how can you find out?

One sure way to find out is to count every calorie you eat for a week and then check your weight to see if you gained or lost pounds during that time.

Every pound is 3,500 calories. If you gained half a pound in one week, you ate 1,750 excess calories.

So if you take the total number of calories you ate for the week and subtract 1,750, you'll know how many calories your body burned in a week. Divide that figure by 7 for your daily calorie requirement.

You can also use calorie calculators to estimate your daily calorie requirement. They can be found online by searching for "calorie calculators" or "estimate calorie requirements."

The estimates from calorie calculators will vary, but they all take into account your level of physical activity. If you are "very active," your body will require more calories than if you are "sedentary."

You might as well tell the truth to the calculator and get the real number. If you don't exercise, you don't exercise. You're not going to change for some calculator.

You can still lose a pound a week by cutting five hundred calories per day out of your diet. Everyone will think you've been working out, and really, isn't that just as good?

"I never did very well in math —
I could never seem to persuade the
teacher that I hadn't meant my
answers literally."

    — Calvin Trillin

5
How to Count Calories

It's a real pain to count calories, but if you use a computer on a daily basis, it can be made a little easier.

There are software programs that will count calories for you if you tell them—honestly—everything you eat and drink.

One useful little program is called Personal Trainer One from SLShareware, Inc. It helpfully includes a database of nearly every kind of food, including menu items from the major fast-food chains.

If you don't want to use a computer, you can count calories with a legal pad and a pen. Write down everything you eat and drink. To make it really easy, eat and drink packaged foods that have the calorie count printed on the label.

Calorie counts for different foods and beverages are available in many places online. The U.S. Department of Agriculture has a complete nutritional database on its web site at **www.usda.gov**. Or check any bookstore for a calorie-counting guide, like *The CalorieKing Calorie, Fat & Carbohydrate Counter,* for example.

It's a good idea to buy a food scale so you know if you're eating three ounces of steak or six ounces of steak or sixteen ounces of steak. With a little practice, you'll be able to judge the portion size without the scale.

Remember, you can eat whatever you want, as long as you keep the total daily calories under your calorie budget.

There's no need to cut out carbs, or go vegetarian, or eat nothing but nonfat food. Eat what you like. Count what you eat. Stop when you get to the magic number.

Once you know how many calories you can eat and still lose weight, you may develop a new appreciation for rice cakes and sliced carrots.

Or maybe not.

You want to find the balance that works for you. No one else can decide what you want to eat. It depends on your schedule, it depends on your mood, it depends on how much you want a chocolate dessert or a glass of wine.

After all, you're not five years old. You don't need assigned snacks. A nap, maybe. But you can pick out your own snacks.

"I went to a restaurant that serves
'breakfast at any time.' So I
ordered French Toast during the
Renaissance."

— *Steven Wright*

6
Eating Out

The great thing about counting calories is that you find out
quickly you can stop eating a lot of things you didn't want
anyway.

If you ever went into a restaurant and ordered a salad
when you really wanted a steak, you may not have been
dieting at all. A salad with cheese and bacon, or raisins and
nuts, or avocado and croutons, doused liberally with salad
dressing, could easily have more calories than a lean 8-ounce
steak.

So have the steak, if that's what you want.

Restaurants can be difficult when you're counting calories.
It's a good idea to stay away from anything they put on the
table before your meal arrives. Watch out for bread, especially

garlic bread. It's not hard to eat 400 calories worth of bread without thinking about it.

Watch out for mixed drinks, too. The syrupy mixers in cocktails can pack 80 calories or more into just 3 ounces, and a typical drink glass holds 8 to 12 ounces.

Two ounces of an 80 proof alcoholic beverage will set you back 128 calories.

So a festive drink at the bar before dinner can easily exceed 300 calories, and if there's a long wait for a table, you might have two.

Now you're into this evening for 600 calories, plus the nuts and pretzels at the bar, and if you have two pieces of bread before dinner, you're pushing a thousand calories and you haven't even eaten yet.

So here are some tips for eating in restaurants while still losing weight:

♦ Have a diet soda at the bar, or drink wine, or drink something on the rocks with just a splash of mixer.

♦ Don't eat the bread unless you really want it.

♦ Stay away from the soup and have the salad. Get the dressing on the side and drizzle it lightly. Don't eat the croutons unless you can't resist.

♦ Order fish, chicken, or steak, grilled or broiled. Stay away from anything with a filling or a sauce.

♦ Beware of vegetables that taste too good. They might be swimming in melted butter. Eat them if you like them, but don't force them down because you think they're good for the diet.

If you go out for breakfast, be aware that anything cooked in a pan probably has 200 calories worth of melted butter in it. Egg dishes, hash browns, bacon, and cheese are not your friends. Pancakes aren't too bad if you skip the butter, go very easy on the syrup, and don't eat more than two of them. Coffee cakes and other baked goods could easily have 400 calories in a fist-sized serving. The good news is that if you've been eating bran muffins or carrot cake because you thought they were healthy, you can stop now.

If you must have breakfast in a restaurant, the best thing to order is probably an egg-white omelette without cheese or bacon. Ask for sliced tomatoes instead of potatoes and order dry toast with butter or preserves on the side. An eight-ounce glass of orange juice contains about 110 calories. Fresh fruit is a good choice, especially if you're on an expense account.

"I keep reading between the lies."
    — *Goodman Ace*

7

Where Calories Hide

It's very helpful to have nutritional information on the side of every packaged food sold in America, and if you can read small print, it's even better.

For example, if you buy a single-serving bottle of a typical mocha cappuccino beverage, the label may inform you that the product contains 65 calories per serving. Look closer, and you may also learn that the single-serving bottle contains 2.5 servings.

It just *looks* like a single-serving bottle.

It looks *a lot* like a single-serving bottle.

If it *were* a single-serving bottle, it would contain 195 calories per serving.

Unless you're pouring this beverage into a toy tea set and serving it to your imaginary friends, this bottle does not serve two and a half people.

Read those labels carefully. An apparently single-serving bag of caramel corn with peanuts, the kind with the prize inside, actually contains 3.5 servings at 140 calories each.

A frozen pizza that serves two people if they're not very hungry may claim to be five servings of 330 calories each.

Don't expect yourself to have the will power to stop eating pizza or caramel corn when you're hungry and it's right there in front of you.

You'll lose more weight if you don't buy that stuff.

Pretzels are better than caramel corn. Turkey is better than pizza.

Mocha cappuccinos are the enemy.

Eat whatever you want, but count whatever you eat. And don't forget to read those labels.

"I've had a perfectly wonderful evening. But this wasn't it."

— *Groucho Marx*

8
I'm Still Hungry

It is very frustrating to total up the number of calories you've consumed during the day and find that you've reached your limit when it's only 9:00 p.m. and you're hungry.

There are two ways to approach this situation.

One is to recognize that you're a night owl, you're going to stay up late, and you're going to eat at night regardless of any diet advice anybody else has ever given you.

In this case, all you have to do is find breakfast foods that are very low in calories, or skip breakfast altogether, so you can have enough room in your calorie budget for late-night snacks.

The other way to address the situation is to find very low calorie late-night snacks.

The important thing is to do what works for you, not what works for someone else. It doesn't matter when you eat, it doesn't matter what you eat. The only thing that matters, for weight loss, is that you eat fewer calories than your body burns.

You don't have to do the same thing every day. Make it easy on yourself.

Here's a tip if you find that your low-calorie diet leaves you feeling unsatisfied: buy a pint of heavy cream to keep in your refrigerator. A teaspoon of heavy cream in a cup of coffee or a bowl of oatmeal is a big improvement, and just that little bit will help you feel full for only about 20 extra calories.

"I don't exercise. If God wanted me to bend over, he'd have put diamonds on the floor."

— Joan Rivers

9

The Unhappy Truth about Exercise

Whatever the health benefits of exercise, the truth is that it probably won't burn enough calories by itself to make you lose weight.

You can walk on a treadmill for thirty minutes and it's barely going to burn enough calories to offset a chocolate chip cookie.

Still, you can lose a pound a week by burning 500 calories per day more than you eat just as you can lose a pound a week by eating 500 calories per day less than you burn.

The choice is yours.

How many calories you burn with exercise depends on your exact weight and your own body, but here are some numbers to give you a rough estimate:

♦ An hour of low-impact **aerobics** will burn about 295 calories if you weigh 130 pounds, about 430 calories if you weigh 190 pounds.

♦ You will burn about 325 calories by riding a **stationary bicycle** moderately for an hour if you weigh 130, about 475 calories if you weigh 190.

♦ **Running** 10 miles in an hour will burn about 945 calories if you weigh 130, about 1,380 if you weigh 190.

♦ **Walking** at a moderate pace for an hour will burn about 200 calories if you weigh 130, about 300 calories if you weigh 190.

♦ Moderate **weight-lifting** burns about 175 calories an hour if you weigh 130, about 260 calories if you weigh 190.

♦ A one-hour **boxing** match will burn 700-1,000 calories, but your health insurance probably doesn't cover plastic surgery, so think about that before you step into the ring.

*"Excess generally causes reaction,
and produces a change in the
opposite direction...."*

　　— Plato

10
More about Exercise

Ice is good for sore muscles, but not more than 20 minutes every hour.

Heat can be helpful. Sports creams and heating pads will ease tightness.

A little bit of gentle stretching is useful.

Anti-inflammatory medicines like aspirin, acetaminophen and ibuprofen will relieve pain. Read the labels and take only as directed.

"I tried every diet in the book. I tried some that weren't in the book. I tried eating the book. It tasted better than most of the diets."

— *Dolly Parton*

11
All Booked Up

At some point you're probably going to get tired of counting calories. It can be annoying to spend your time writing it all down and counting it all up.

When you start to feel that way, you can always drop by a bookstore and browse through the diet books section, where you'll find lots of different approaches to losing weight.

You could try *The Zone*, or *The Fat Smash Diet*, or *Eating For Life*, or *You: On A Diet*.

Maybe you prefer to seek a doctor's advice with *Dr. Atkins' New Diet Revolution* or the even newer *The All-New Atkins Advantage*. There's also that old stand-by from Irwin Stillman, *The Doctor's Quick Weight Loss Diet*, and don't be surprised to find *The Complete Scarsdale Medical Diet* on the shelf right next to it.

You can diet by body part with the *Flat Belly Diet* and *The Abs Diet*, or by climate with *The Mediterranean Diet* and *The South Beach Diet*, or by the calendar with *The Two-Day Diet*, or *The 4 Day Diet*, or *The 5-Day Miracle Diet*, or *The 30-Day Low-Carb Diet Solution*.

If you don't crave a lot of variety, you might like *The New Cabbage Soup Diet* or *The Grapefruit Solution*.

Or perhaps you'd like to get in touch with your inner Darwin and try *The Evolution Diet*, or *The Paleo Diet*, or *NeanderThin: Eat Like a Caveman*.

They'll all work, if you can stick with them.

Maybe Jackie Gleason said it best. "The second day of a diet is always easier than the first. By the second day, you're off it."

*"I have gained and lost the same
ten pounds so many times over and
over again my cellulite must have
déjà vu."*

— Jane Wagner

12
Why You Yo-Yo

In the entire history of aviation, no test pilot ever achieved greater velocity than the sound-barrier-shattering speed with which weight returns to your hips after you lose it.

The miserable phenomenon of the yo-yo diet is easily explained.

Let's say you're female, 5 feet, 5 inches tall, 35 years old, and weigh 160 pounds. Let's say you don't exercise at all, you work at a desk, and your parking space is close to the door. Your body will burn about 1,780 calories per day.

Now let's assume you're the same person doing the same things, but you've lost 40 pounds. Your new, lighter body will only burn about 1,570 calories per day.

That means if you eat exactly what you ate before you lost 40 pounds, the same diet that kept your weight stable back then is going to put weight on you now at the rate of approximately half a pound per week.

Remember, you gain a pound for every 3,500 calories you consume over what your body burns, so if you're eating 210 calories per day more than your body burns, it only takes sixteen and two-thirds days to gain a pound. In two years you will have gained back the whole 40 pounds, and that's without even enjoying yourself.

Of course, you can gain back the 40 pounds a lot faster if you start to gain weight, get upset with yourself, and then give up in despair because you think you must have some terrible character flaw.

But it's not a character flaw. It's just math. The less you weigh, the fewer calories your body burns.

Don't be discouraged and don't make yourself crazy. There's nothing wrong with you. It's just math.

Eat whatever you want, but count the calories. Then you'll always know where you stand, and you can control your weight with mathematical precision.

It's not the easiest thing in the world, but it works every time.

There's *nothing wrong with you*.

Conclusion

Your own mind is perfectly capable of understanding everything you will ever need to know.

Advertisers and marketers may manipulate you into feeling
confused, alarmed, or afraid to trust your own judgment.

Whenever you catch yourself feeling that way, stop and look
carefully, not at yourself, but at whatever they're trying to
sell you.

Ask yourself how much they spent on that ad campaign or
sales pitch.

Then apply Lincoln's Law: The more money they're spending
to sell it to you, the less you need it.

Enjoy your life and your peace of mind.

There's *nothing wrong with you.*

About the Author

Babe Lincoln lives in Southern California.

In answer to the question most frequently asked, Babe is not short for Babraham. Abe was short for Abelicious.

Additional Reading
and Resources

On the Money

The Little Book of Common Sense Investing: The Only Way to Guarantee Your Fair Share of Stock Market Returns
by John C. Bogle
Wiley, 2007

Vanguard founder John C. Bogle explains how index investing can work for you.

A Random Walk Down Wall Street (Revised and Updated): The Time-Tested Strategy for Successful Investing
by Burton G. Malkiel
W.W. Norton & Co.; Revised and Updated edition, 2007

In this updated version of his 1973 book, Princeton economics professor Burton Malkiel evaluates all kinds of investment opportunities and their suitability for investors of different ages.

Capitalism: The Unknown Ideal
by Ayn Rand, Nathaniel Branden, Alan Greenspan, Robert Hessen
Signet, 1986

The more you learn to trust your own mind, the more you'll appreciate Ayn Rand. This is a collection of short articles first published during the 1960s.

Economics in One Lesson
by Henry Hazlitt
Laissez Faire Books; 50th Anniversary Edition, 2008

Henry Hazlitt's 1946 book demystifies economics and will help you sort out good ideas from bad ones. This updated 50th anniversary edition includes an introduction by Steve Forbes.

The Wall Street Journal. Complete Personal Finance Guidebook
by Jeff D. Opdyke
Three Rivers Press, 2006

Everything you always wanted to know, but it was always so expensive to ask.

Losing It

Hungry Girl: Recipes and Survival Strategies for Guilt-Free Eating in the Real World
by Lisa Lillien
St. Martin's Griffin, 2008
Low-calorie recipes to help you stay under your calorie budget.

Eat Out, Eat Right: The Guide to Healthier Restaurant Eating
by Hope S. Warshaw
Agate Surrey; 3rd edition, 2008
Advice on what to eat when you're not the one doing the cooking.

The CalorieKing Calorie, Fat & Carbohydrate Counter 2009
by Allan Borushek
Family Health Publications, 2008
All the numbers to help you count calories.

The Calorie King Food & Exercise Journal
by Allan Borushek
Family Health Publications, 2006
A little more help with calorie counting.

DietMinder Personal Food & Fitness Journal
by F. E. Wilkins
MemoryMinder Journals, Inc.; Revised edition, 2007
More help with calorie counting; this one is a spiral-bound diary.

Eat This, Not That! Supermarket Survival Guide: The No-Diet Weight Loss Solution
by David Zinczenko, Matt Goulding
Rodale Books, 2008
Helpful tips for grocery shopping.

Eat This, Not That! Thousands of Simple Food Swaps that Can Save You 10, 20, 30 Pounds—or More!
by David Zinczenko, Matt Goulding
Rodale Books, 2007
Tips on cutting calories without giving up eating.

Find It Online

You can find calorie-counting programs to run on your computer by going to your favorite Internet search engine and searching for "calorie counting software" or just "calorie counting."

There are web sites specializing in "shareware," programs that are available free or for very low license fees. Try searching on **www.download.com** for "calorie counting." Don't forget to read the system requirements for the programs before you download and install them. Get the version that will work with your computer and operating system.

Software like **Personal Trainer One** will run on your computer even if you're not connected to the Internet. Alternatively, you can use an online calorie-counter that doesn't require any software installation, like the free online calorie-counting program at **http://caloriecount.about.com**.

The Diet Shelf

The Zone: A Dietary Road Map to Lose Weight Permanently : Reset Your Genetic Code : Prevent Disease : Achieve Maximum Physical Performance
By Barry Sears, Ph.D., and Bill Lawren
Collins Living, 1995

The Fat Smash Diet: The Last Diet You'll Ever Need
by Ian K. Smith, M.D.
St. Martin's Griffin, 2006

Eating For Life
by Bill Phillips
High Point Media, LLC, 2003

You: On A Diet:
The Owner's Manual for Waist Management
by Michael F. Roizen, M.D., and Mehmet C. Oz, M.D.
Free Press, 2006

Dr. Atkins' New Diet Revolution, Revised Edition
by Robert C. Atkins, M.D.
M. Evans, 2003

The All-New Atkins Advantage: The 12-Week Low-Carb Program to Lose Weight, Achieve Peak Fitness and Health, and Maximize Your Willpower to Reach Life Goals
by Stuart L. Trager, M.D., and Colette Heimowitz, M.Sc.
St. Martin's Griffin, 2008

The Doctor's Quick Weight Loss Diet
by Irwin M. Stillman, M.D.
Dell, 1987

The Complete Scarsdale Medical Diet: Plus Dr. Tarnower's Lifetime Keep-Slim Program
by Herman Tarnower, M.D., and Samm Sinclair Baker
Bantam, 1982

Flat Belly Diet
by Liz Vaccariello and Cynthia Sass, M.P.H., R.D.
Rodale Books, 2008

The Abs Diet: The Six-Week Plan to Flatten Your Stomach and Keep You Lean for Life
by David Zinczenko and Ted Spiker
Rodale Books, 2005

The Mediterranean Diet
by Marissa Cloutier, M.S., R.D., and Eve Adamson
Harper, 2004

The South Beach Diet: The Delicious, Doctor-Designed, Foolproof Plan for Fast and Healthy Weight Loss
by Arthur Agatston, M.D.
St. Martin's Griffin, 2005

The Two-Day Diet
by Tessa Cooper, M.S., and Glenn Cooper, M.D.
Ballantine Books, 1995

The 4 Day Diet
by Ian K. Smith, M.D.
St. Martin's Press, 2008

5-Day Miracle Diet
by Adele Puhn, M.S., C.N.S.
Ballantine Books, 1997

The 30-Day Low-Carb Diet Solution
by Michael R. Eades, M.D., and Mary Dan Eades, M.D.
Wiley, 2003

The New Cabbage Soup Diet
by Margaret Danbrot
St. Martin's Paperbacks, 2004

The Grapefruit Solution: Lower Your Cholesterol, Lose Weight and Achieve Optimal Health with Nature's Wonder Fruit
by Daryl L. Thompson and M. Joseph Ahrens, Ph.D.
LINX Corp., 2004

The Evolution Diet: What and How We Were Designed to Eat, Second Edition
by Joseph Morse
Code Publishing, 2008

The Paleo Diet: Lose Weight and Get Healthy by Eating the Food You Were Designed to Eat
by Loren Cordain, Ph.D.
Wiley, 2002

NeanderThin: Eat Like a Caveman to Achieve a Lean, Strong, Healthy Body
by Ray Audette and Troy Gilchrist
St. Martin's Press, 1999